FAMILIES

BY MARTI ABBOTT AND BETTY JANE POLK

FEARON TEACHER AIDS
Simon & Schuster Supplementary Education Group

Editor: Carol Williams
Copyeditor: Cynthia Seagren
Illustration: Tom McFarland
Design: Diann Abbott

ISBN 0-8224-1351-5

Printed in the United States of America
1. 9 8 7 6 5 4 3 2 1

Contents

Gift (Language Arts) • Furniture Frenzy (Language Arts) • Label Lookers (Health) • Super Salutations (Social Studies)

Synopsis • Introduction • Critical-Thinking and Discussion Questions • Creative Writing Starters (Language Arts) • Cinquain Sentiments (Language Arts) • Paper Quilt (Art) • Name Banners (Art) • Falling Stars (Science)

Introduction

All too often teachers read a book to children to entertain them or fill some spare moments, and that is the end of it. With the closing of the book, teachers shut out children's responses and ideas. Teachable moments are lost forever. The Books and Beyond series provides teachers with creative activities and critical-thinking stimulators to maximize the effectiveness of good literature. A piece of literature can become the basis for a learning unit that spans many areas of the curriculum.

Each lesson in the Books and Beyond series begins with a brief synopsis of the book and introductory ideas to stimulate student interest. After reading the book aloud, the use of the critical-thinking and discussion questions will help children draw from their own related experiences and analyze, evaluate, and apply the message of the book. Follow-up activities that center around many curriculum areas and include a variety of teaching styles will help children move beyond the book and internalize its message.

Families is a collection of lessons based on children's books designed to familiarize children with a variety of family structures. Children will naturally relate to the stories of sibling rivalry and learn valuable lessons from the stories dealing with families in crisis. Combine parents and grandparents. Mix together a few brothers and sisters. Stir well and add a carload of relatives, and you have the perfect recipe for family fun.

A Chair for My Mother

Written and illustrated by Vera B. Williams
New York: Greenwillow Books, 1982

Synopsis

After a fire destroys their home and everything they own, a little girl, her mother, and grandmother begin saving to buy the one thing they can afford—a new chair. They each contribute the money they earn to a large jar. The big day finally arrives when the jar will not hold another coin and they set off to buy a "wonderful, beautiful, fat, soft armchair." This Caldecott Honor book is an inspiring story of starting over and family comradery.

Introduction

Ask children if they have ever saved to buy something they really wanted. Ask children how long it took them to save and if they were satisfied when they finally made their purchase. Encourage children to listen closely as the story is read aloud to find out how this family saves money and what they plan to buy.

Critical-Thinking and Discussion Questions

1. The little girl in the story knew her mother would love to have a "wonderful, beautiful, fat, soft armchair" to relax in after work. So she helped save money to buy a chair. If you had a jar full of coins, what would you like to buy? Who would you buy this object for?

2. The little girl recalls the day that a big fire burned up everything in her house. How do you think the little girl and her mother felt when that happened? Have you ever lost or ruined something you really liked? How did you feel?

3. What are some ways the neighbors and other family members helped out when the little girl, her mother, and her grandmother moved into their new apartment? Have you ever helped someone out when they had a problem? What did you do? Have you ever given something of yours to someone who needed it more than you? What was it?

4. How long do you think it took to fill the jar full of coins? Do you think the little girl, her mother, or grandmother ever felt discouraged? Do you ever feel discouraged when you have to wait a long time for something you really want?

5. The family really enjoyed the armchair after they purchased it. It was just right. Do you think they will refill the jar with coins to make another purchase? What do you think they will save for this time?

Creative Writing Starters
Language Arts

In my family, we help each other by _____ .
I would like to save money to buy _____ .
If our family had to start over, we would probably _____ .

Story Titles
Starting Over
My Best Purchase
Special Savings

Be a Good Neighbor
Language Arts

When the family moved into their new apartment, the neighbors and relatives helped out by bringing rugs, curtains, dishes, and beds. Encourage children to think about ways they could be good neighbors and help out those in need around them. Help children realize that the term "neighbor" is not limited to the people who live right next door. "Neighbors" can include anyone they come in contact with—the person sitting next to them in class, a family member, teacher, or friend. Give each child a sheet of lined paper. Invite the children to write paragraphs explaining who they have chosen as their "neighbor" and how they plan to help them out. Encourage children to actually carry out their plans and then to share with the class what they did.

Interior Decorating
Art

The little girl in the story wanted to buy a chair covered in velvet with roses all over it. Encourage children to imagine what kind of chair they would like to buy. Give each child a copy of the "My Favorite Armchair" reproducible on page 12. Invite children to decorate the chair using crayons, watercolors, or markers and then cut it out. Give each child a 12" x 18" sheet of construction paper and invite children to draw an entire room in which to place their favorite armchair. Encourage children to think about what colors, designs, and patterns would look good together. When the room is complete, have children glue the cut-out chair in place on the paper.

Counting Coins
Math

It must have been a big job for the family in *A Chair for My Mother* to count all the coins they had saved in the jar. Draw a large circle on the chalkboard and label it "nickel, 5¢." Draw a smaller circle and label it

"penny, 1¢." Draw another circle smaller still and label it "dime, 10¢." Play a coin counting game with the children. Point to the dime drawn on the chalkboard and have the class tell you how much it is worth. Point to the dime again and have children add to the amount they said before and give the new total. Continue pointing to the dime while children count by tens. Try the same exercise pointing to the nickel and have children count by fives each time you point to the coin. To make the game more challenging, point to a combination of coins beginning with the largest amount. For example, point to the dime three times, the nickel twice, and the penny five times. If the children count aloud correctly as you point, they will say, "Ten, twenty, thirty, thirty-five, forty, forty-one, forty-two, forty-three, forty-four, forty-five."

Fire Safety
Social Studies

Review the importance of fire prevention and practice fire-safety procedures that have been established at your school. Encourage each child to initiate a family meeting at home to discuss a home fire drill. Invite a local firefighter to come visit the classroom to give the children helpful information and answer questions regarding fire safety.

Name _____

My Favorite Armchair

Decorate the armchair with your favorite colors and designs.

Families © 1991 Fearon Teacher Aids

Hazel's Amazing Mother

Written by Rosemary Wells
New York: Dial, 1985

Synopsis

Hazel heads out on a simple errand, but soon takes a series of wrong turns and is completely lost. Hazel and her beloved doll, Eleanor, meet up with three bullies. As the bullies grab Eleanor, Hazel helplessly watches them destroy the beloved doll her mother made for her. Hazel's amazing mother rescues her in a most unique and imaginative way.

Introduction

Ask children what they think the word *amazing* means. Encourage children to give examples of things or experiences that they consider to be amazing. In the story, Hazel thinks her mother is amazing. Invite children to listen closely as the story is read aloud to find out why Hazel's mother is so special.

Critical-Thinking and Discussion Questions

1. Hazel's mother made Hazel a beautiful doll named Eleanor. Describe how Eleanor looked. Hazel was very fond of Eleanor. Has anyone ever made anything especially for you? Who? Describe how the special gift looked.
2. Hazel made several wrong turns on her way back home. She ended up on a lonely hilltop in a part of town where she had never been before. How do you think Hazel felt? Have you ever been lost? How did you feel? What did you do?
3. Hazel was powerless to stop the bullies from destroying her beautiful doll. Have you ever felt that you had no power to change a situation? When? What would you have done if you had been Hazel? Why?
4. Hazel's first reaction after her doll had been ruined and the carriage splashed into the pond was to call for her mother to help her. Who do you call for help when you are in trouble or are feeling sad?
5. Mothers and fathers are wonderful people to have around, but even they are not able to always make everything happen the way we might like. What parts of this story do you think are make-believe? What parts do you think are real? Why?

Creative Writing Starters

Language Arts

I feel helpless when _____.

The best thing to do if you are lost is _____ .

I wish someone could have rescued me the day that _____ .

Story Titles

Wrong Turn

Mom to the Rescue!

The Unpredictable Picnic

Help the Mailman

Language Arts

Hazel stopped to help the mailman while she was on her errand. Remind children that they can help the mailman by learning how to correctly address the envelopes carrying the letters that they mail. Draw a large envelope on the chalkboard and explain the parts of the address:

Name

Number and Street Name (Apt. #, if necessary)

City, State   Zip Code

Explain that the person sending the letter writes his or her own address in the upper left-hand corner of the envelope and that this is called the return address. Explain the purpose of having a return address. The address of the person to whom the letter is being sent is written in the lower right quadrant of the envelope. Give each child an envelope and invite children to practice correctly addressing several letters. Have children write their addresses as the return address and the school address as the mailing address.

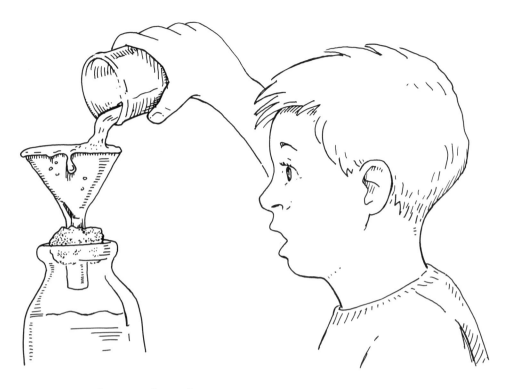

That's Amazing!

Science

A great wind sprang up and blew the picnic blanket with Hazel's mother in it up into the sky. The blanket filled with air, ballooned out, and sailed over town. Although this is a make-believe part of the story, air can have tremendous force and power. Show children a scientific experiment that demonstrates the force air pressure can have. Place a funnel in the opening of a clear glass bottle. Using modeling clay, make a tight seal around the bottle opening. (The seal *must* be airtight.) Pour water into the funnel. If the seal is airtight, the water will amazingly remain in the funnel and not flow into the empty bottle. The air inside the bottle is not able to escape. The air pressure inside the bottle prevents the water from leaving the funnel. Break the seal and the water will gush into the bottle.

Pack a Picnic

Health

Show children the picture in *Hazel's Amazing Mother* that shows Hazel and her mother enjoying the food they packed for their picnic. Ask children what they would pack in a picnic basket. Remind children of the importance of eating balanced meals that include foods from each of the four basic food groups. Give each student a copy of the "Pack a Picnic" reproducible on page 17. Invite children to pack their picnic baskets choosing from the pictured foods at the bottom of the page. Encourage children to choose one food from each food group.

Wrong Turn

Social Studies

Students can practice following navigational directions (north, south, east, and west) playing this board game. Make a game board by dividing a 7" square of construction paper into a grid of 49 one-inch squares. Color the center square to indicate the starting point on the board and write the letter *N* in the center square at the very top of the board to indicate north. Divide children into groups of three students each and give each group a 7" game board and a copy of the reproducible on page 18. (Reproduce the cards on construction paper so the cards will be sturdier.) Have children cut the cards apart and put them face-down in a stack. Each player places his or her marker (bean, macaroni, or button) in the center square to begin the game. Each player draws a card from the stack and moves the marker according to the directions on the card. On the player's next turn, he or she moves the marker from the spot where it was left after the last turn. Eventually the directions will cause the players to fall off the edge of the game board. The winner of the game will be the player who is last to take a "wrong turn" and fall off the board.

Pack a Picnic

Pack your picnic basket with a balanced lunch. Choose one food from each food group. Cut the pictures out and glue them on the basket in the correct spot.

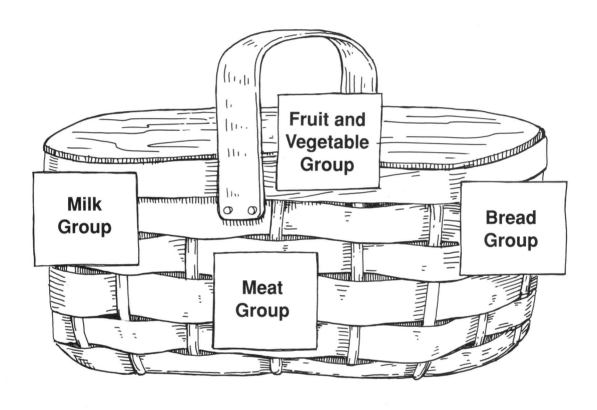

Families © 1991 Fearon Teacher Aids

Wrong Turn

Cut the cards apart and put them in a stack with faces down.

South 2 spaces	**North** 2 spaces	**South** 1 space	**West** 1 space	**East** 2 spaces
West 2 spaces	**North** 1 space	**East** 3 spaces	**South** 3 spaces	**East** 1 space
Northeast 1 space	**Northwest** 2 spaces	**Southeast** 1 space	**Southwest** 2 spaces	**Northeast** 2 spaces
Northwest 1 space	**Southeast** 2 spaces	**Southwest** 1 space	**Any direction!** 2 spaces	**Any direction!** 3 spaces

Families © 1991 Fearon Teacher Aids

Ox-Cart Man

Written by Donald Hall and illustrated by Barbara Cooney
New York: Viking Press, 1979

Synopsis

A New England family works hard through the seasons spinning yarn, making candles, growing potatoes, and splitting shingles. They work together to have their wares ready for market. The family loads the ox-cart and father makes the trip to Portsmouth where he sells the goods. The family then begins the cycle again in preparation for another yearly trip.

Introduction

Ask the children to tell about a time when they worked together with their families on a project. Ask children to tell what their role was. Ask children what jobs they do around their homes. Explain to children that the family in this story works together all year on a very special project. Invite the children to listen closely as the story is read aloud to find out what the project is and how it turns out.

Critical-Thinking and Discussion Questions

1. The ox-cart man and his family packed the ox-cart with the things they had made or grown all year long to sell at the Portsmouth Market. What were some of the things they packed in the ox-cart? What are some things your family could make or grow to sell at a market?

2. The ox-cart man traveled alone to Portsmouth. How long did it take him to get there? Do you think he got lonely? Why do you think his wife and children did not go with him? Would you have liked to travel along with the ox-cart man? Why or why not?

3. The family in the story lived in New England. They grew or made everything they had and they traveled by ox-cart. How is this family different from your own? Are there any ways in which you would like your family to be more like this one? What ways?

4. This New England family earned the money they needed by selling what they had made or grown. How does your family earn money? Do you earn money? How?

5. Each member of the family worked very hard to do his or her share of the work. How does your family work together? Which of the jobs mentioned in the story would you have liked most? What jobs do you do to help your family? Is there a job you do not like to do? Is there a job that you wish you could do? What?

Creative Writing Starters
Language Arts

I help my family by _____ .
Our family works together when we _____ .
The best way to earn money is to _____ .

Story Titles
A Day at the Market
The Best Job in the World
The Ox-Cart Upset

All's in Order
Language Arts

Ask children to name the items the ox-cart man sold at the market. Make a list on the chalkboard. When the list is complete, invite the class to work together to put the list in alphabetical order. Ask the first volunteer to come up to the chalkboard and write the numeral 1 beside the item that would come first in alphabetical order. Invite a second volunteer to identify the item that would come second and write the numeral 2 beside it. Continue until all the items have been numbered and "all's in order."

Candle Creations
Art

The ox-cart man and his family made many things from the supplies they had available to them. One such item they made was candles. Divide the class into groups of five or six students to make dip candles. Put some chopped wax (any color) into a juice can for each group. Set the juice can in a pan of water. Heat the water over very low heat to melt the wax. Be sure each group has adult supervision. When the wax is melted, turn the heat off. Give each group a piece of 10-ply cotton twine a bit longer than the depth of the melted wax in the juice can. Invite group members to dip the twine into the melted wax. Leave about $1/2"$ at the top to hold on to and to serve as the wick once the candle is made. Children should wait about five seconds between each dip. A small candle about $3/8"$ will require about 125 dips. Invite each group member to take a turn dipping the candle into the melted wax until the candle reaches the desired size.

Crayon Cross-Stitch
Art

The daughter in the story embroidered linen during the winter as one of her jobs. Ask children to bring in some samples of embroidery or cross-stitch from home to show the class. Children can make cross-stitch patterns using graph paper and crayons. Give each child a piece of graph paper and invite children to outline a simple geometric shape or design. Children can use different colors of crayons to fill in the design by making an X in each square inside the outline.

Market Math

Math

The family in the *Ox-Cart Man* sold the items they had made or grown for a profit. But the story doesn't tell how much money the items sold for or how much profit the family made. Ask children to speculate about how much money they think the family might have made. Give each child a copy of the "Market Math" reproducible on page 22. Invite children to read each question carefully and answer the hypothetical math problems.

Market Math

Carefully read and answer each word problem.

1. The ox-cart man had five pairs of mittens to sell. He was paid $1.25 for each pair. How much money did he make if he sold all five pairs? _____

2. The potatoes sold for 5¢ a pound. The ox-cart man sold 100 pounds. How much money did he get for the potatoes? _____

3. The ox-cart man could sell his honey for 50¢ a jar. He sold 20 jars of honey. How much money did he make selling his honey?_____

4. The ox-cart man had five birch brooms to sell. He sold each one for $1.00. How much money did he make selling the brooms?_____

5. The family had made twelve boxes of candles. Each box sold for $3.00. How much money did the family make selling the candles? _____

6. The ox cart sold for $20.00. The ox sold for $25.00. The harness sold for $5.00. How much did the man make selling the cart, ox, and harness?_____

7. The apples sold for $10.00. The goose feathers sold for $4.00. The linen sold for $7.00 and the man got $6.00 for the wool. How much did the man make all together after selling these four items?_____

Families © 1991 Fearon Teacher Aids

Daddy

Written by Jeannette Caines and illustrated by Ronald Himler
New York: Harper & Row, 1977

Synopsis

Windy looks forward with great anticipation to her daddy's visits every Saturday. They spend the day together laughing, playing hide-and-seek, coloring, and making chocolate pudding. During the week, Windy sometimes gets "wrinkles" in her stomach worrying about her daddy. But each Saturday morning when she answers the door and sees her daddy waiting with a warm hug, the "wrinkles" go away.

Introduction

Ask children to remember a time when they were excitedly waiting for something that was going to happen—a birthday party, holiday, or vacation. Explain to children that the little girl in the story can hardly wait for Saturdays to arrive. Invite children to listen closely as the story is read aloud to find out what makes Saturdays so special.

Critical-Thinking and Discussion Questions

1. Windy and her daddy laughed and played together. What are some of the things they enjoyed doing together on Saturdays? What do you like to do on Saturdays? Who do you like to do these things with?
2. Windy looked forward to her daddy's visit each Saturday. Looking forward to something is part of what makes the event so special. What do you look forward to doing? How do you feel when you know you are planning to do something special?
3. How do you think Windy would have felt if her daddy did not come to visit her one Saturday? Do you think that will ever happen? Why or why not? Has anyone ever promised you something that they did not do? How did you feel? Do you always do what you say you are going to do?
4. Windy said that she gets "wrinkles" in her stomach before her daddy comes to get her and when she worries about him. What do you think "wrinkles" are? Do you ever get "wrinkles" in your stomach? Why?
5. Although Windy's daddy does not live with her, he loves her very much. How can you tell that Windy's daddy loves her? How can you tell that Windy loves her daddy? Who are the people you love and look forward to spending time with?

Creative Writing Starters
Language Arts

I like to spend my Saturdays with _____ .
Sometimes I pretend that I am _____ .
I look forward to _____ .

Story Titles
The Great Eyeglass Finder
Brown Bag Surprise
The Shaving Cream Clown

Wrinkles
Language Arts

Windy got "wrinkles" in her stomach when she worried about her daddy. Ask children what they worry about. Help children realize that everyone has worries and concerns. The important thing is to find constructive ways to deal with the worries—to iron out the "wrinkles." Give each child a sheet of lined writing paper. Encourage children to describe some of the "wrinkles" they sometimes feel in their stomachs. Invite volunteers to read their papers aloud and encourage other children to help with ideas for ironing out the "wrinkles." For example, students may get "wrinkles" in their stomachs when they think about taking a test at school. Discuss ways to relieve that type of anxiety, such as studying carefully and realizing that trying your best is what really counts. Extend the lesson by having children recopy their "wrinkles" on the top half of a sheet of lined paper and write the solution to dealing with the "wrinkle" on the bottom half of the page. Crease (or wrinkle) the page diagonally to divide it into two sections. Display the neatly written pages on a bulletin board entitled "Ironing Out the Wrinkles."

Label Detectives
Language Arts and Math

In the story, Daddy and Windy had to read the labels on the shelves at the supermarket for Paula because she didn't wear her glasses when she went out. Give each student a copy of the "Read the Label" reproducible on page 27. Encourage children to look carefully at the front and back of the cereal box at the top of the page. Invite children to be label detectives by carefully answering the questions.

Shaving Cream Creations
Art

Daddy and Windy made their faces look like clowns using shaving cream. Children can have lots of fun using shaving cream to design patterns, pictures, and silly faces. Have each student remove everything on his or her desktop so it is completely clean. Squirt a small dollop of shaving cream on each desktop. Add a drop or two of food coloring to the shaving cream dollop to create a colorful dimension to the creations. Invite children to spread the shaving cream with their hands and create fingerpaint designs. When children are finished, have them use their hands to scrape as much of the shaving cream off the desk as their hands can hold. Have children wash their hands in a sink or dip them in a bucket of water. Wipe the remaining shaving cream off the desktops with a sponge.

Calendar Connections

Math

Windy knew her daddy would not forget to visit her each Saturday because he wrote the date on his calendar. Give each child a copy of the "Calendar Connections" reproducible on page 28. Read over the calendar together and then invite children to answer the questions.

Name _____

Read the Label

Look carefully at the front and back of the cereal box and answer each question.

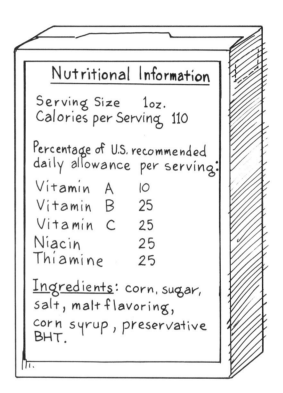

1. What is the name of the cereal? _____

2. How many ounces (oz.) are in each serving?_____

3. If each person ate one ounce of cereal, how many people would the box serve? _____

4. If you ate one serving of Corn Crispies, what percentage of the daily allowance of Vitamin C would you get? _____

5. What are the first three ingredients in Corn Crispies?

_____

6. How many calories are in two servings of Corn Crispies? _____

7. Is there more Vitamin A or Niacin in this cereal? _____

Name _____

Calendar Connections

Look carefully at the plans written on the calendar. Answer each question.

JUNE

SUNDAY	MONDAY	TUESDAY	WEDNESDAY	THURSDAY	FRIDAY	SATURDAY
		1	2	3	4	5
6	Piano lesson 3:30 ♫ 7	8	9	Dentist appointment 2:00 10	11	Go to the beach with Sara 12
13	Piano lesson 3:30 ♫ 14	15	Meet Pete at the library 5:00 16	17	Have dinner at Sue's 6:00 18	19
Meet Tom at Roller World 4:00 20	Piano lesson 3:30 ♫ 21	22	23	Clean bird cage 24	25	26
27	Piano lesson 3:30 ♫ 28	29	30			

1. On what day each week do you have a piano lesson?_____

2. What time do you plan to meet Pete at the library? _____

3. You checked out some library books on the 16th. They are due in two weeks. Put a star on the calendar to show the day you will need to return the books.

4. What plans did you make for the third Friday of the month?

_____

5. If a friend called and asked you to come over at 3:30 on Sunday the 20th, what would you say?_____ Why?_____

_____

Families © 1991 Fearon Teacher Aids

Daddy

Nobody Asked *Me* If I Wanted a Baby Sister

Written and illustrated by Martha Alexander
New York: Dial Books, 1971

Synopsis

Oliver resents his new baby sister. He puts Bonnie in his wagon and sets off to find a new home for her. Just as Oliver is about to leave his sister with a new family, Bonnie's reaction causes Oliver to have a change of heart and a new attitude towards the situation.

Introduction

Ask the children if they have ever been given something they didn't want. Encourage children to tell what they did with the unwanted gift. Explain to children that the little boy in this story has something he doesn't want. Invite the children to listen closely as the story is read aloud to find out how Oliver handles the situation.

Critical-Thinking and Discussion Questions

1. Oliver had a scowl on his face when he first realized he had a new baby sister. Why do you think he was so unhappy? Do you have a younger brother or sister? How did you feel about him or her at first? Why?
2. Oliver tried to give his new sister away. Do you think that was a good solution to the problem? Why or why not? Why did the people Oliver ask refuse to take his sister? What would you have said if someone asked you if you wanted a "beautiful, chubby baby?" Why?
3. When Toby's mother held the baby, it cried. Toby's mother wondered if the baby were hungry or if a pin were sticking her. What are some other reasons a baby cries?
4. Bonnie stopped crying when Oliver held her. How do you think that made Oliver feel? Oliver told Bonnie that she was a lot smarter than he thought. What do you think Oliver meant by that? How do you think Oliver's opinion of his baby sister changed?
5. Oliver started to make plans to play "horse and wagon" with his sister when she got older. What are some other things that Oliver and Bonnie could enjoy doing together? What are some things you enjoy doing with your brothers, sisters, or friends?

Creative Writing Starters
Language Arts

If I had a baby sister, I would _____ .
I like to _____ with my brothers and sisters.
Babies often cry when _____ .

Story Titles
Nobody Asked Me
The Great Giveaway
The Worst Thing About My Sister/Brother

What Is and What I Wish
Language Arts

Show children the last page of *Nobody Asked Me If I Wanted a Baby Sister* and explain that the realistic picture on the bottom of the page portrays "what is" and the picture inside the bubble portrays what Oliver wishes were true. Give each child a copy of the "What Is and What I Wish" reproducible on page 32. Invite each child to draw a realistic picture of him or herself interacting with a brother or sister. Encourage children who have no siblings to draw a picture of themselves interacting with a parent or friend. Have children draw a picture in the bubble showing what they *wish*. Invite children to share their pictures with the class and to explain what is happening in both situations.

Ask Me
Language Arts

Oliver was upset because nobody asked him what he thought about adding a new member to the family. Everybody likes to feel that their opinions, likes, and dislikes are valued. Give each student a copy of the "Ask Me" reproducible on page 33. Invite students to pair up with a partner and complete the surveys. Encourage partners to interview each other and record the answers.

Are You My Mother?
Science

Oliver finally decided not to give his baby sister away to another mother. Encourage children to think of some funny, mixed-up mother/baby animal combinations. Reinforce the names of animals and their young by playing a bingo game. Give each child a copy of the reproducible on page 34 and some bingo markers, such as buttons, beans, or macaroni. Write the animal names in Column A on the chalkboard. Have children copy one name in each box on their bingo cards in random order.

A	B
horse	foal
cow	calf
cat	kitten
dog	puppy
frog	polliwog
hen	chick
goat	kid
goose	gosling
rabbit	bunny

Call out the name of one of the baby animals in Column B. Students find the name of the animal's mother on their card and place a marker in that square. Continue calling names of baby animals until one student has placed markers in a row horizontally, vertically, or diagonally on the card and calls out "Bingo."

Baby Care
Social Studies

Set up a dramatic-play center equipped to provide children with opportunities to dramatize proper infant care. Provide dolls, diapers, bottles, washcloths, spoons, empty baby food containers (unbreakable), and blankets. Demonstrate some ways Oliver could help care for his new baby sister using the materials and a doll. Leave the materials out in the play area and invite children to practice caring for a small infant.

What Is and What I Wish

Draw a picture of a real situation between you and a family member or friend at the bottom of the page. Draw a picture in the bubble of the same people in a situation as you *wish* it could be.

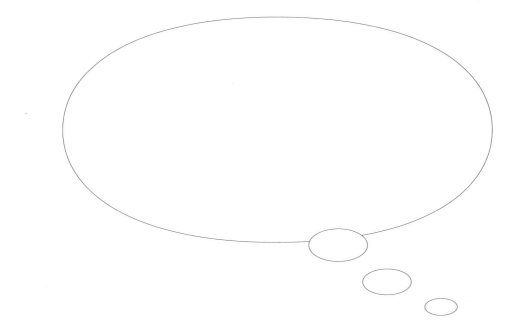

Families © 1991 Fearon Teacher Aids

Nobody Asked *Me* If I Wanted a Baby Sister

Interviewer _____

Ask Me

Ask your partner the questions on the survey and write down his or her answers.

☐ 1. What is your full name?_____

☐ 2. How old are you? _____ When is your birthday? _____

☐ 3. What is your favorite dessert? _____

☐ 4. What do you think is the most important thing a person should learn? _____
_____

☐ 5. What is your favorite sport? _____

☐ 6. What would you like to change about your family?_____
_____

☐ 7. What do you think is the perfect age? Why?_____

☐ 8. What would you like to win a trophy for doing?
_____

☐ 9. Would you like to have a new brother or sister? _____ Why or why not? _____
_____

☐ 10. What would you like to do or be when you grow up?
_____

Are You My Mother?

Nobody Asked *Me* If I Wanted a Baby Sister

Families © 1991 Fearon Teacher Aids

The One in the Middle Is the Green Kangaroo

Written by Judy Blume and illustrated by Amy Aitken
New York: Bradbury Press, 1981

Synopsis

Freddy feels unimportant as the middle child. He desperately searches for something to do that no one else in his family has ever done. Freddy finally has a shot being center stage as the Green Kangaroo in the school play. After taking a bow at the end of his performance and hearing the audience clap loud and hard, Freddy realizes how special he really is.

Introduction

Ask children to think about what makes them feel special. Some children may think of many things, while others may have a difficult time. Explain to children that the little boy in the story does not feel special at all. Invite the children to listen closely as the story is read aloud to find out why Freddy does not feel special and how he solves his problem.

Critical-Thinking and Discussion Questions

1. Freddy saw some disadvantages of being the middle child in his family. What place are you in your family? What are the disadvantages of being in that place? Are there any advantages? What?

2. Freddy wished desperately that he could do something that no one else in his family had ever done before. He thought that being in the school play was the perfect opportunity to make that wish come true. What would you like to do that no one in your family has ever done before?

3. Mike choked on his potato and knocked over a whole glass of milk when he heard the news that Freddy was going to be the Green Kangaroo in the school play. Why do you think he reacted this way? Have you ever been surprised by some news someone told you? How did you react?

4. What do you think was going through Freddy's mind when he first stepped out on the stage the evening of the play? Have you ever stood in front of a group of people? How did you feel?

5. At the end of the story, Freddy no longer cared that he had to wear Mike's hand-me-down clothes. It no longer bothered him that he had to share a room with Mike. He didn't even care much about being the one in the middle. Freddy felt good just being Freddy. What do you think caused his attitude to change? Do you feel good about just being you? Why or why not? If not, how can you change the way you feel?

Creative Writing Starters

Language Arts

I feel special when _____ .

If I had a chance to perform in front of a crowd, I would like to _____ .

I dream about being a _____ .

Story Titles

My Big Debut

Center Stage

The Strange Green Creature

Feeling "Center Stage" Special

Language Arts

Freddy felt good when he first stepped out on stage and realized that he was the center of attention. He was no longer in the middle. He was all by himself and he had an important job to do. Encourage children to share times they have felt as special as Freddy did the evening of the play. Invite children to think of one thing they would like to do that would make them feel special. Some children may, like Freddy, like the chance to be center stage to recite a poem, sing a song, or show some other special talent. Other children may feel special if they have the opportunity to have a private one-on-one appointment to talk with their favorite teacher or the principal. Some children may feel special if they are assigned an important job or task. After each child has decided on what will make him or her feel special, carry out each child's wish on a special day assigned just to that child.

What Did You Say?

Language Arts

Ms. Gumber told Freddy to "break a leg" before he went out on stage. Freddy thought she meant that he should fall off the stage and really break his leg. The phrase "break a leg" really means "good luck" to actors and actresses. We use other phrases, called *idioms*, that have special meanings. Idioms are phrases or expressions whose total meaning together differ from the meaning of the individual words. Write the following idioms on the chalkboard and discuss their meanings.

in the same boat	catch your breath
fish out of water	let it all hang out
break the ice	miss the boat
have a ball	nip it in the bud
eager beaver	spill the beans

Invite each student to choose one idiom and copy it at the top of a sheet of lined paper. Encourage students to write a paragraph explaining the idiom or to write a short story in which the idiom is used.

The Grass Is Always Greener

Social Studies

Each child in your class can probably give you reasons why they would like to be in someone else's position in a family. Middle children, like Freddy, will relate easily to his complaints. Oldest children, youngest children, and even only children will be able to state the disadvantages of their positions. Encourage children to think about the advantages of their birth order. Help children realize that everyone has problems that need to be worked out. Invite children to think of constructive ways to deal with their problems, just as Freddy did. Put children in discussion groups according to their birth order. Put all oldest children together, only children, and so on. Encourage groups to name some advantages and disadvantages of their birth order and list them on a sheet of paper.

Big Leapers
Physical Education

Kangaroos are known as "big leapers." One leap can carry the animal three or four times its own length and a kangaroo can easily sail over a fence its own height. Have children stand behind a line and each take a turn broad jumping as far as they can. Measure the distance each child jumps and encourage children to try to beat their own records. Place two jump ropes parallel to one another (12" apart) on a soft indoor or outdoor surface. Invite each child to take a running start and jump over the two ropes in one leap. After each child has had a turn, slightly widen the gap between the two ropes to encourage children to leap again to clear the ropes in one bound. Continue widening the gap between the two ropes until the "kangaroos" reach their leaping limit!

My Brother Fine with Me

Written by Lucille Clifton and illustrated by Moneta Barnett
New York: Holt, Rinehart and Winston, 1975

Synopsis

Baggy is tired of his Mama and Daddy always telling him what to do. Running away seems to be the perfect solution. Johnetta thinks her life will be problem-free if her little brother Baggy would leave, and so she helps him pack. After Baggy leaves, Johnetta begins to realize how much she misses Baggy. It may not be easy having a younger brother around, but it's no fun *without* one either.

Introduction

Ask each child to share with the class how many brothers or sisters they have living in their home, or if they are the only child in their family. Ask children if they have ever wanted to change the size of their family. Explain to children that the little girl in the story has an idea of how changing her family would make her life better. Invite children to listen closely as the story is read aloud to find out if Johnetta is happy with the change.

Critical-Thinking and Discussion Questions

1. Baggy felt like running away from home because he was tired of his Mama and Daddy always telling him what to do. Do you ever get tired of people telling you what to do? Have you ever considered running away? Do you think running away is a good solution to a problem? Why or why not?

2. Johnny thought her only problem was her brother, Baggy. She thought if he ran away everything would be great. What do you consider your biggest problem at home? What do you think would make that problem go away?

3. Johnny was mad for a long time when she first realized she would have a younger brother. How do you feel about your brothers and sisters? Are you glad that you have them around? Are there times when you feel like Johnny and wish they would run away? Why? If you are the only child in your family, do you wish you had siblings, or are you glad you are alone?

4. Baggy dreamed of running away to a place where he could have his own minibike. If you could travel to a perfect place, what would be waiting there for you when you arrive?

Creative Writing Starters
Language Arts

My life at home would be better if only _____.
I feel like running away when _____ .
The thing I like most about my family is _____ .

Story Titles
My Family Fine with Me
No Fun Alone
My Only Problem

Sandwich Samplers
Language Arts

Ask children to raise their hands if their favorite sandwich is the same as Baggy's. Encourage children to watch closely as you make a peanut butter and jelly sandwich. After you have finished, ask children to name in sequence the steps they observed. Give each child a copy of the "Make a Sandwich" reproducible on page 43. Invite children to list the supplies needed to make a peanut butter and jelly sandwich on the top half of the paper and to write sequential steps for actually making the sandwich on the bottom half. Collect the papers and choose one. Make another sandwich in front of the class following the exact directions on the student's page you chose. Choose several children to come to the front of the room and make a sandwich following a set of directions written by a classmate. Children will begin to realize the importance of writing specific directions and the demonstrators will get a lesson in how to follow directions.

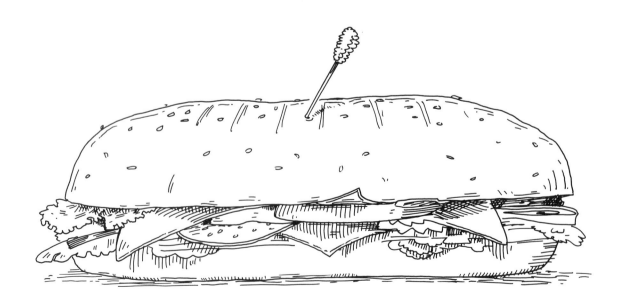

Home Alone
Safety

Baggy and Johnny had to "see after the house" while Mama and Daddy were at work. Many children are home alone after school while their parents are working. Take this opportunity to remind students of some safety procedures to keep in mind when home alone. Invite children to do some role playing to practice handling situations, such as a phone call or a knock on the door.

"My Family Fine with Me" Mobiles
Art

Give each child a coat hanger and a copy of the "My Family Fine with Me" reproducible on page 44. Invite children to cut out each rectangular piece and draw a picture of one family member on each. Children who have large families will need more than one copy of the reproducible. Using a hole punch, have children punch a hole at the top of each figure and the "My Family Fine with Me" banner. Encourage children to write one reason why each family member is "fine" with them on the back of each figure. Invite children to use yarn to hang the figures and title banner from the coat hanger to make their own unique family mobiles.

Let Freedom Ring
Social Studies

Just after Baggy leaves, Johnny says, "Now he done run away, and I feel just like Dr. King say, free at last." Ask children if they can explain what Johnny meant by that. Explain that Martin Luther King, Jr., was a leader of the civil rights movement in the United States in the 1950's and 1960's. He spoke out for the black Americans who were not receiving fair treatment. Under his leadership, unfair laws were abolished. In one of his speeches delivered from the Lincoln Memorial in Washington, D. C., Dr. King said that he hoped one day freedom would ring from every mountainside. Ask children if they can think of other events in history that allowed freedom for a particular group of people (Declaration of Independence, Emancipation Proclamation, and so on). Encourage children to think about the freedoms they have living in America that they might not have if they lived elsewhere in the world.

Name _____

Make a Sandwich

What you need:

What you do:

My Family Fine with Me

Families © 1991 Fearon Teacher Aids

Brothers Are All the Same

Written by Mary Milgram and illustrated by Rosmarie Hausherr
New York: E.P. Dutton, 1978

Synopsis

Nina, Kim, and Joshie are all members of the same family. But Rodney, the boy next door, says Joshie is not a real brother because he is adopted. Nina and her friends set out to show Rodney that brothers are all the same.

Introduction

Hold up a pen and a pencil for the children to see. Ask the children if the two objects are alike or different. Most students will probably say that the two objects are different because of their appearance. But point out that although the objects look different, they are alike in that they are both writing instruments and can accomplish the same task. Invite the children to listen closely as the story is read aloud to find out how brothers and sisters are both different and alike.

Critical-Thinking and Discussion Questions

1. Rodney thought he knew everything. Nina and Kim disagreed. Do you ever think that you know everything? Are you willing to learn new things from your friends? What have you most recently learned from a friend that you didn't know before?
2. Why do you think Rodney acted like he knew everything even when the girls showed him that he was wrong?
3. The children began to tell about "dumb" things their brothers had done. Joshie jumped in the bathtub with his clothes on and Marcia's little brother tried to brush his teeth with shaving cream. Have you ever made a silly mistake? What did you do? Did you laugh when you realized your mistake or did it make you angry? Why?
4. Sometimes brothers, sisters, and friends say things that make you feel sad. Rodney's brother called him a "second-grade baby." Rodney reacted by calling his brother "dumb." Has anyone ever said something to you that hurt your feelings? Did you say something mean back to them?
5. Rodney realized that even though there are many types of brothers and ways of getting them, a brother is still a brother. Do you think brothers and sisters "are all the same"? Why or why not?

Creative Writing Starters
Language Arts

The silliest thing I ever did was _____ .
When someone says something mean to me, I _____ .
Sometimes my friends and I argue about _____ .

Story Titles
A Different Kind of Family
Always Right
I Never Knew

Outrageous Actions
Language Arts

In the story, Nina and her friends began discussing some of the silly things their brothers had done to prove to Rodney that all brothers are the same. We have all done silly things from time to time—some by accident and some just because they were fun! Give each child a copy of the "Silly Sam" reproducible on page 49. Invite children to fill in the missing words in the story about Silly Sam to describe his outrageous actions. Encourage children to think of creative and unique answers. Children can read the stories aloud to the class or draw pictures to complement the stories.

Twins

Language Arts

The children in the story found ways that they thought all brothers were the same. Group the children in pairs and give each pair a copy of the "Twins" reproducible on page 50. Invite children to look carefully at the worksheet to find pairs of brothers that look identical. Have children cut the pictures apart and place them face down on a table or desktop. Children can play a game of "concentration" by trying to match the twins. One player turns over two cards to see if they match. If the cards match, the player keeps them and continues to play. If no match is made, the player turns the cards back over face down. The player with the most pairs of twins at the end of the game is the winner.

Paper Airplanes

Art and Science

The children in the story enjoyed making paper airplanes together. Rodney realized that there were a hundred ways to make an airplane. Give each child a sheet of drawing paper and encourage children to fold, crease, and cut the paper to make a unique airplane. *The Paper Airplane Book* by Seymour Simon (New York: Viking Press, 1971) is an excellent resource. Incorporate the basic principles of flight (drag, lift, thrust, and gravity) in your discussion to help children improve their designs.

Who's the Leader?

Physical Education

This game improves coordination and observation skills. The object is to look like everyone else. Invite the children to stand in a big circle. Choose one student to leave the room and then designate one of the remaining students in the circle to be the leader. The leader begins an action, such as clapping, and all other players in the circle join in. Invite the child who left the room to come back. That child's job is to figure out who the leader is by carefully observing. The leader can change actions at any time. The others in the circle must, as quickly as possible, copy the action and join in. The leader may choose to hop on one foot, do jumping jacks, and so on. Remind students not to stare at the leader so his or her identity will remain a mystery. Once the leader has been identified, choose a different student to leave the room and designate a new leader.

Silly Sam

Fill in the blanks to complete the story about Silly Sam.

Silly Sam does crazy things. He takes a bath in a tubful of _____ . Sam brushes his teeth with _____ . He rides a _____ to school. Sam carries his lunch to school in a _____ . Sam never needs to sharpen his pencil because he writes with a _____ . At recess, Silly Sam plays jump rope using a _____ and he kicks a _____ instead of a soccer ball. After school, Sam does his homework while he _____ and he watches _____ instead of TV. Sam uses a _____ to eat his dinner. And, at the end of a long day, Sam crawls into his _____ to go to sleep.

Name _____

Name _____

Twins

Cut the cards apart. Match the pairs of brothers that look alike.

Brothers Are All the Same

Families © 1991 Fearon Teacher Aids

The Relatives Came

Written by Cynthia Rylant and illustrated by Stephen Gammell
New York: Bradbury Press, 1985

Synopsis

This Caldecott Honor book tells the amusing story of a station-wagon-full of people who leave Virginia one summer on a trip to visit their relatives. Though tired and wrinkled upon arrival, hugs abound and the good times begin. The relatives hug, eat, and breathe together for weeks and weeks. After the relatives leave, the house seems too quiet and the beds too big, but next summer is not that far away.

Introduction

Ask children if they have ever had a guest stay at their house. Ask children to imagine what it might be like if they had ten guests visiting at one time. Invite the children to listen closely as the story is read aloud to find out what happens when a house is overflowing with relatives who come for a visit.

Critical-Thinking and Discussion Questions

1. The relatives left Virginia at four in the morning when it was still dark to begin their trip. Why do you think they left so early? Have you ever left that early for a trip? Where were you going?
2. The relatives traveled in the car all day and into the night. What are some things they did to pass the time? What do you like to do to entertain yourself when you go on a long trip in a car?
3. The relatives greeted each other with lots of hugs. Who do you like to hug? How do you feel when someone hugs you? What other ways can you show someone you care about them?
4. The relatives stayed for weeks and weeks. Although there was not a lot of extra room in the house, they all enjoyed each other. Have you ever had someone stay at your house as a guest? Who? Did you enjoy their visit? Why or why not? Who would you like to have come visit you?
5. After the relatives left, the beds felt "too big and too quiet." What do you think that means? What are some other ways the hosts' house would seem different after the relatives left?

Creative Writing Starters
Language Arts

I would like to have _____ come visit me.

It is fun to _____ in the car on a long trip.

If we had guests at our house, we would need extra _____ and _____.

Story Titles

The Relative Invasion

One Hundred Hugs

The Bumpy Ride

Pack a Suitcase
Language Arts

Ask children what they think the relatives might have packed in their suitcases. Ask children what they would pack in their suitcases if they were going on a trip. Give each child a copy of the "Pack a Suitcase" reproducible on page 55. As a vocabulary extender, invite children to think of something to pack in their suitcases that begins with each letter in the word *relatives*. Children might enjoy brainstorming ideas in small groups.

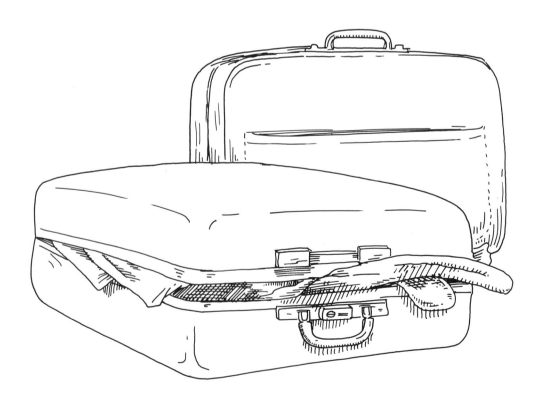

Going to the Relatives
Language Arts

This is an excellent whole-class or small-group game to help improve listening and sequencing skills. Have the children sit in a circle. One child begins the game by saying, "I am going to the relatives and I will take _____. " The child fills in the blank with the name of an item that begins with the letter A. The child seated to the first child's right continues the game by repeating what the first child said and then completing the sentence with the name of an item that begins with the letter B. For example, the second child might say, "Randy is going to the relatives and he is taking *a*pples. I am going to the relatives and I am taking *b*alloons." The third child repeats what the first two children have said and then completes the sentence naming an item that begins with the letter C. The game continues until every child in the circle has had a turn. Begin playing the game with small groups. Increase the difficulty of the game by playing with more and more children in one circle.

Cooperative Collage
Art

The relatives shared and cooperated with one another to make the visit more enjoyable. They shared their food and beds. They cooperated by working together to accomplish tasks. The relatives helped "tend the garden and they fixed any broken things they could find." Invite children to work in pairs to make a "Cooperative Collage." Provide each pair of children with a sheet of construction paper, magazines, glue, and scissors. Encourage children to cut out pictures from the magazines that show people sharing and cooperating with one another. Have the children glue the pictures on the sheet of construction paper. Display the collages on a bulletin board.

Tracking the Trip
Social Studies

The relatives left Virginia before daybreak and didn't arrive at their destination until they had driven "all day and into the night." Ask children to speculate about where they think the relatives were going. Give each child a copy of the "Tracking the Trip" reproducible on page 56. Help children locate Virginia and the state where they live on the map. Help children chart possible routes between the two places. Invite children to choose a state they would like to visit and chart a route to that destination.

Pack a Suitcase

Pack your suitcase by writing an item that begins with each letter in the word *relatives*.

R _____

E _____

L _____

A _____

T _____

I _____

V _____

E _____

S _____

Name _____

Tracking the Trip

1. What state do you live in? _____
   Color your state green.

2. Color the state of Virginia purple.

3. Draw a line between your state and Virginia to track your trip.

4. Write the names of all the states you would pass through on
   your way from your state to Virginia. _____

_____

_____

_____

_____

The Relatives Came

Freddy My Grandfather

Written and illustrated by Nola Langner
New York: Four Winds Press, 1979

Synopsis

Freddy's granddaughter gives a biographical description of her unique Hungarian-born grandfather. She knows what he likes, what makes him angry, and most important, that she loves him very much.

Introduction

Ask children to think of a family member or friend. Then ask children to share what they think is the "best thing" about that person. Explain to children that the little girl in the story describes her grandfather and what he is like. Invite the children to listen closely as the story is read aloud to find out what the little girl thinks is the "best thing" about Freddy.

Critical-Thinking and Discussion Questions

1. How would you describe the relationship between Freddy and his granddaughter? Do you have a similar relationship with a family member or friend? Who?
2. The little girl admitted that she sometimes worried. She worried one time when there was a big storm with lightning and thunder. What do you worry about? The little girl ran around and then tried to hide from the storm. What do you do when you are worried?
3. Freddy helped his granddaughter face her worry by coming to the window and looking at the sky light up during the storm. Freddy helped her see the beauty of the lightning and she felt better. Do you know someone who helps you see the bright side of dark situations? Who?
4. Freddy's granddaughter thought Freddy was young, although her mother told her that her grandfather was pretty old. Why do you think the little girl thought her grandfather was "pretty young"? What do you think makes a person seem young?
5. The little girl watched her grandfather's every move. She knew what he liked, what made him angry, and she understood everything he said. What do you think the little girl learned from watching her grandfather? What have you learned from watching what other people do?

Creative Writing Starters
Language Arts

I sometimes worry about _____.
I love the smell of _____ because it reminds me of _____ .
I know _____ is angry with me when _____.
Story Titles
My Grandfather
Stranger in a New Country
Forever Young

Person Profiles
Language Arts

Freddy's granddaughter knew her grandfather very well. She had observed him closely and she knew his likes, dislikes, mannerisms, and habits. The little granddaughter also knew that she loved her grandfather very much. Encourage children to think of a family member that they love and understand very well. Give each child a copy of the "Person Profile" reproducible on page 61. Invite children to complete the profile about the family member they have chosen. Children can introduce their family member to the class by reading the profile aloud when it is completed. Display profiles on a bulletin board entitled "People in Profile."

Tailor-Made
Math

Freddy once had a tailor shop and he loved to sew. A tailor would need to know how to measure carefully. If a garment is being made to fit a particular person, the tailor would need to get that person's exact measurements to be sure the garment would be the right size. Give each child a copy of the "Tailor-Made" reproducible on page 62. Have children cut away the centimeter strips and tape or glue them together to make a measuring tape. Have children work with a partner to measure and record their answers.

Smelling Snoop
Science

Freddy's granddaughter loved the smell of Freddy's room. It smelled like cigars and lemons. Ask children to name some of their favorite smells. Encourage children to think about why the scents are their favorites and if the scents remind them of someone or something. Invite children to do some investigative work using only their sense of smell. Place a cotton ball saturated with lemon juice in an empty film container or other small opaque container with a lid. Open the lid and ask for volunteers to smell the container and guess the scent. Try the same activity using other familiar scents, such as cinnamon, vanilla, talcum powder, laundry detergent, or perfume.

Hungarian Goulash
Social Studies

Freddy was unique to his granddaughter because he was Hungarian. Point out Hungary on a world map. Show a picture of the Hungarian flag. A famous Hungarian soup is a thick stew called goulash. It is made with cubes of beef and seasoned with paprika. Invite the children to help you prepare the following recipe.

Hungarian Goulash

2 pounds round steak (cut into $1/2$ inch cubes)

1 c. chopped onion

1 clove garlic (minced)

2 T. flour

1 tsp. salt

$1/2$ tsp. pepper

1 $1/2$ tsp. paprika

$1/4$ tsp. dried thyme (crushed)

1 bay leaf

1 14 $1/2$ ounce can tomatoes

1 c. sour cream

Put steak cubes, onion, and garlic in a crock pot. Stir in flour and mix to coat steak cubes. Add all other ingredients, except sour cream. Stir well. Cover and cook on high 3 to 4 hours, stirring occasionally. Add sour cream 30 minutes before serving. Serve over hot buttered noodles.

Name _____

Person Profile

Choose a family member or friend that you would like to write about. Write his or her name in each box and then fill in the blanks.

┌──────────────────────────────┐
│   │   • • •
└──────────────────────────────┘

grew up in _____.

gets angry when _____.

likes to _____.

makes me mad when _____.

likes to visit _____.

wears _____.

is crazy about _____.

loves to _____.

always says _____.

is happy when _____.

But the best thing about  is

_____.

Families © 1991 Fearon Teacher Aids

Tailor-Made

Cut the centimeter strips from the side of the page. Tape or glue the four strips together. Ask a partner to help you measure accurately.

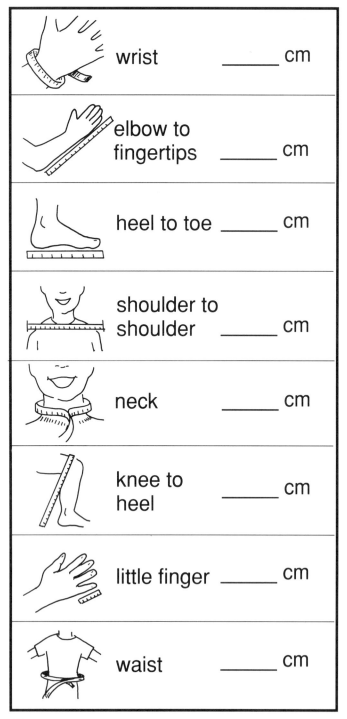

wrist _____ cm

elbow to fingertips _____ cm

heel to toe _____ cm

shoulder to shoulder _____ cm

neck _____ cm

knee to heel _____ cm

little finger _____ cm

waist _____ cm

	glue here	glue here	glue here
80			
79	59	39	19
78	58	38	18
77	57	37	17
76	56	36	16
75	55	35	15
74	54	34	14
73	53	33	13
72	52	32	12
71	51	31	11
70	50	30	10
69	49	29	9
68	48	28	8
67	47	27	7
66	46	26	6
65	45	25	5
64	44	24	4
63	43	23	3
62	42	22	2
61	41	21	1

Me and My Aunts

Written by Laura P. Newton and illustrated by Robin Oz
Niles, Illinois: Albert Whitman & Company, 1986

Synopsis

A little girl tells about the unique qualities of each of her five aunts. She admires and loves them all, but she has a special fondness for the aunt that she calls the "Rememberer." This aunt remembers what it is like to be a child and can understand some of the special feelings that young children experience.

Introduction

Ask children if they think they have good memories. Do a memory testing exercise. Say five numbers in a row and ask the children to repeat the same five numbers back to you. Do a clapping pattern and ask the class to repeat this pattern for you. Explain to children that one of the aunts in the story has an especially good memory. Invite children to listen closely as the story is read aloud to find out what kinds of things the aunt remembers.

Critical-Thinking and Discussion Questions

1. The little girl in the story enjoyed all of her aunts, but the one she liked best of all was the aunt who was a "Rememberer." This aunt remembered what it was like to be a little girl. Which of your relatives do you enjoy the most? Why?
2. If you had the same five aunts that the little girl in the story had—a baker, a seamstress, a teacher, a traveler, and a "Rememberer"—which one would you most enjoy? Why?
3. The aunt who was the "Rememberer" understood what it was like to be frightened during a thunderstorm, to be without a best friend, and to imagine. Do you have any feelings that you wish an adult could remember and understand? What?
4. The little girl wanted to learn to do some of the things her aunts could do. She was learning to sew and bake. Do you know someone who can do something that you would like to learn to do? Who? What would you like to learn from them?
5. At the end of the story, the little girl says that when she is an aunt she will try to remember, too. What do you think she meant by that? What kinds of things do you think she will remember?

Creative Writing Starters
Language Arts

The relative I most enjoy is _____ because _____ .
I want to grow up to be just like _____ because _____ .
_____ understands me the best.

Story Titles
Memory Failure
My New Talent
A New Day

Remember When
Language Arts

Prepare a transparency for the overhead projector with several shapes or simple picture outlines (square, house, ball, flag, tree, and so on). Project the transparency on the wall using an overhead projector so that all the children can see it. Give children 15 seconds to carefully study the items projected. Remove the transparency at the end of the 15 seconds and give each child a sheet of writing paper. Ask children to recall as many items as they can and write them down on the sheet of paper. After completing the remembering exercise, ask children to speculate about why we remember some things and don't remember others. Ask children why they think the aunt in the story remembered so well what it felt like to be a child. Encourage children to think about a memory they have of their past. Invite some children to share their memories aloud with the class. The memory may be a happy, sad, or a frightening first-time experience. Give each child a sheet of writing paper. Encourage children to write a paragraph or short story describing their memories.

Champion of the World
Language Arts

The niece in *Me and My Aunts* thought her aunts were all champions at what they did. She admired their talents. Encourage children to think of something at which they consider themselves to be champions or at which they would like to become the best in the world. Give each child a 3" yellow construction paper circle and two 1" x 4" blue construction paper strips. Invite children to make a medal for themselves by writing "World's Best _____" on the yellow circle and attaching the two blue "ribbons." Invite children to attach the medal to the upper left corner of a sheet of lined paper and write a story about how they became the best in the world at what they do, their experiences as a champion, or how they are using their talent to help others.

Gifts from Around the World
Social Studies

The aunt who was the traveler sent gifts to her niece from all around the world. The story said that this year the aunt would be traveling to China. Ask students to guess what gift the aunt will bring back from China. Give each student a copy of the "Gifts from Around the World" reproducible on page 66. Invite children to match the gifts with the appropriate countries by writing the country's name on the line below each package.

Name _____

Gifts from Around the World

Match each gift with the country from which it came. Write the name of the country on the line below each package.

India   Holland   Australia   Mexico

Japan   France   Germany   Italy

kimono

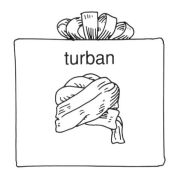
turban

lederhosen

_____   _____   _____

kangaroo

beret

_____   _____

sombrero

wooden shoes

spaghetti

_____   _____   _____

Me and My Aunts

Families © 1991 Fearon Teacher Aids

The Wednesday Surprise

Written by Eve Bunting and illustrated by Donald Carrick
New York: Clarion Books, 1989

Synopsis

Each Wednesday, Anna and her grandma get together with a big, lumpy bag filled with books. They are planning a special surprise for Dad's birthday. Finally the Saturday of Dad's birthday arrives. The family gathers for the big occasion. After all the other gifts have been presented to Dad, Anna and Grandma present their Wednesday surprise—the best birthday gift of all.

Introduction

Show children the cover of the book and ask them to guess what they think the Wednesday surprise might be. Chances are good that no one will correctly identify the answer. Explain to the children that they will be surprised when they find out what the secret is all about. Invite the children to listen closely as the story is read aloud to find out what the big surprise is.

Critical-Thinking and Discussion Questions

1. It seems that most often older family members help younger ones. But in this story, Anna helps her grandma learn to read. Have you ever helped an older family member do something? Who? What did you help them do?
2. Grandma and Anna had a surprise that they were trying to keep a secret until Dad's birthday. Have you ever had a secret? Was it hard to keep? What was your secret?
3. Grandma and Anna enjoyed reading books together. Do you enjoy reading? Who do you like to read books with? What is your favorite book?
4. Why do you think Grandma had never learned to read when she was younger?
5. Do you think it was hard for Anna to teach her grandma to read? Do you think you could teach someone to read? Why or why not? What do you think is the hardest part about learning to read?
6. What are some things you read every day? How would your life be different if you could not read?

Creative Writing Starters
Language Arts

I think reading is important because _____ .
I would like to teach someone how to _____ .
My favorite book is _____ .
Story Titles
Saturday's Surprise
Saving the Best for Last
When Grandma Winks

Bagful of Books
Language Arts

Check out a supply of picture books from your school or local public library and put them in a book bag similar to the one Anna and her grandma used in *The Wednesday Surprise*. Keep the bagful of books handy in the classroom and pull one out from time to time during the week and read it aloud to the class. Encourage each child to get a public library card. Give each child a copy of the "_____'s Reading Record" reproducible on page 71. Invite children to keep a record of the books they read over the next month. At the end of the month, ask children to choose one of their favorite books and be prepared to share some information about their books. Invite children to give a brief synopsis of the book and then read their favorite pages aloud to the class, just as Anna's grandma read aloud to her family.

A Complete Week
Language Arts

Divide the children into groups of three students each to play a game that will reinforce the days of the week. Give each child a copy of the "A Complete Week" reproducible on page 72. Each player cuts out the playing card (the section divided into sevenths) and the days-of-the-week squares. Give each group a paper sack and have players put all the days-of-the-week squares into the bag. Each player takes a turn by drawing a square from the bag and placing it in the correct spot on his or her playing card. The first slot of the playing card is for Sunday, the second for Monday, and so on. The starred square on the playing card is for Wednesday. Wednesday was a special day for Anna and her grandma and it is a special day in this game, too. Each time a player draws a square that says "Wednesday" they get to draw another square. When a square is drawn that is already filled on the playing card, the square is returned to the bag and the player's turn is over (unless the

player drew a "Wednesday" square, in which case the player can draw again). The first player to correctly fill his or her playing card is the winner.

Reading Poster
Art

Remind children of the importance of reading. Ask children to name some things they read every day (traffic signs, cereal boxes, labels, and so on). Discuss good reading habits, proper care of books, and important library procedures. Give each child a 12" x 18" sheet of construction paper. Invite children to design posters that will help promote good reading habits or remind others of important practices concerning the library or the care of books. Display the finished posters around your classroom or school.

Breath Pictures

Science

Anna made a breath picture while she waited for her grandma. Help children understand the concept of condensation by conducting a simple experiment. Fill a clear glass with colored water and add several ice cubes. Set the glass aside. Take a close look at the glass about an hour later. Encourage children to describe any changes they observe. (They will observe that the outside of the glass is wet.) Explain that the moisture on the outside of the glass is not from the water inside the glass (or it would be colored water), but it is from the air that is surrounding the outside of the glass. When warm air comes in contact with the cold glass, it condenses to form water droplets. Relate the discovery to the breath picture Anna made on the window.

_____'s
Reading Record

BOOK TITLE	AUTHOR	DATE FINISHED

A Complete Week

Cut apart the worksheet on the dotted line. Cut the days-of-the-week squares apart and put them in a paper bag.

			★			

- -

Wednesday	Tuesday	Tuesday	Tuesday	Wednesday
Thursday	Thursday	Thursday	Sunday	Sunday
Monday	Monday	Monday	Saturday	Saturday
Wednesday	Friday	Friday	Friday	Wednesday

The Wednesday Surprise

The Tenth Good Thing About Barney

Written by Judith Viorst and illustrated by Erik Blegvad
New York: Atheneum, 1971

Synopsis

A little boy, with the help of his parents, begins to understand the death of his cat. Barney is remembered fondly at a cat funeral, and Father explains that change is inevitable and can be very positive. In time, the little boy's sadness begins to go away.

Introduction

Ask children with pets to tell about the characteristics of their pets that they enjoy most. Ask if any children have ever had a pet die, and if so, how they felt about it. Explain to the children that in the story a little boy is very sad about the death of his cat, but he remembers the good things about Barney. Invite children to listen closely as the story is read aloud to find out what makes Barney so special.

Critical-Thinking and Discussion Questions

1. The little boy in the story was very sad that his cat, Barney, had died. He cried and didn't feel like watching television or eating. He even cried when he went to bed. Have you ever felt that sad? What made you sad? How did you act?

2. Mother gave the little boy a hug to help him feel better. Who has helped you when you were feeling sad? What did they do? What could you do for someone else who is feeling sad?

3. The little boy's father agreed that Barney's death was sad. He also said that tomorrow it may not seem quite as sad as today. Do you think that is true? Does time help you get over your sadness? Why or why not?

4. After Barney's death, Father explained to the little boy that things change. Barney would no longer be the little boy's pet, but Barney would have another important job. What are some things that have changed in your life?

5. What are some things the little boy did that showed he really loved Barney? How do you show your friends, family members, or pets that you really love them?

Creative Writing Starters
Language Arts

I was very sad when _____ .
When _____ changed, I felt _____ .
When I feel sad, I usually _____ .

Story Titles
Cat Heaven
The Day of Change
A Nice Job for a Cat

Ten Good Things
Language Arts

The little boy found pleasure in remembering the good things about Barney. Encourage children to think about the positive qualities of their pets and other animal friends. Give each child a copy of the "Remembering Good Times" reproducible on page 77. Invite children to think of a pet or animal they have known. Have children draw a picture of the animal and write the animal's name. Then ask them to write sentences about the good times they have had with the animal they have named.

Cat Puppet
Art

Children can make a cat puppet by folding a sheet of paper. Give each child a 9" square of light brown, gray, or white construction paper and two paper clips. Make available a variety of colored construction paper scraps. Have children fold the 9" paper as follows:

1. Fold the square into a triangle. Fold again to make a smaller triangle.
2. Open the sheet of paper. The center of the paper is where the two fold lines cross. Fold each corner into the center to make a smaller square.
3. Turn the square over and fold the corners into the center again to make a smaller square.
4. Fold this square in half with the folded corners inside.
5. Slide your thumb and first three fingers into the four pockets. Put a paper clip at the top and bottom of the puppet to hold the sides together.

Children can add eyes, nose, tongue, and whiskers by gluing on scraps of construction paper. The bottom of the cat's chin can be rounded using scissors. Bend the ears forward.

Ordinal Clues

Math

Give each child a copy of the "Count and Color" reproducible on page 78. Children will need crayons and a blank sheet of paper. Ask children to cover their papers with the blank sheet of paper so that only the first row of pictures shows. Give children the following oral directions for ordinal number practice.

Look at the balloons in the first row.
1. Color the first balloon red.
2. Color the third balloon purple.
3. Draw orange dots on the fifth balloon.
4. Color the eighth balloon yellow.

Move your paper down so you can see the flowers in the second row.
1. Color the fourth flower red.
2. Draw a stem and two leaves on the seventh flower.
3. Color centers of the second and tenth flowers yellow.
4. Draw a circle around the sixth flower.

Move your paper down so you can see the faces in the third row.
1. Draw brown hair around the third face.
2. Draw a baseball cap on the head of the fourth face.
3. Draw ears on the tenth face.
4. Color the eyes blue on the fifth face.

Move your paper down so you can see the houses in the fourth row.
1. Draw a door on the first house.
2. Draw two windows on the eighth house.
3. Draw a fence around the fourth house.
4. Draw a chimney on the third house.

Chart the Changes

Science

Father pointed out that things change in the ground. The father and his son planted seeds in the garden. Give each child a clear plastic cup, several lima beans, and a wet paper towel. Have the children spread the wet paper towel loosely in the cup and then place the lima beans around the cup's sides. Encourage children to watch the seeds over the next few days and notice the changes that occur. Be sure the paper towel is kept moist. Once the seeds have sprouted, transfer them to small cups filled with potting soil and continue to watch the changes. Give each child a sheet of construction paper. Have children fold the paper to make four boxes. As children watch the progress of their mini-gardens, invite them to draw a picture every few days in one of the boxes to chart the changes they observe.

Name _____

Remembering Good Times

Choose an animal that you know really well. Draw that animal's picture in the box. Write the animal's name on the line below the box. Write ten good times you have had with the animal you name.

_____

1. _____
2. _____
3. _____
4. _____
5. _____
6. _____
7. _____
8. _____
9. _____
10. _____

The Tenth Good Thing About Barney

Count and Color

1

2

3

4

Families © 1991 Fearon Teacher Aids

The Tenth Good Thing About Barney

The Terrible Thing That Happened at Our House

Written by Marge Blaine and illustrated by John C. Wallner
New York: Four Winds Press, 1975

Synopsis

Mother goes back to work and the family experiences some drastic changes. This "terrible thing" causes one family member to feel ignored, as if no one is listening anymore. But when the family members begin to work together as a team, things aren't so terrible after all.

Introduction

Show children the cover of the book. Ask children what they would consider to be a terrible thing if it happened at their house. Invite the children to listen closely as the story is read aloud to find out what the terrible thing is in this story and how the family deals with it.

Critical-Thinking and Discussion Questions

1. The little girl considered her mother going back to work a "terrible thing." Do you think it was a "terrible thing"? Why or why not? How would you have felt if you had been in the little girl's situation?

2. The mother said that she was returning to work to be a science teacher because she thought it was important work. What are some other reasons why a parent would want or need to return to work?

3. When the little girl could stand the chaotic situation no longer, she yelled out that no one cared, listened, or would even pass the milk. After her parents realized that she was upset, they listened carefully and then worked on a solution to the problem. What do you think might have happened to this family if the little girl had never expressed how she felt? Do you always tell your family how you are feeling? Why or why not?

4. At the end of the story, the little girl says that her mother and father were "real" parents after all. What do you think she meant by that? Do you consider your parents "real"? Why or why not?

5. The family enjoyed talking together, playing games, and going to the park. What are some things you enjoy doing with your family? Has there ever been a time when you could not enjoy doing your favorite things with your family because of a "terrible thing"? When?

Creative Writing Starters
Language Arts

My favorite time with my family is _____ .
A terrible thing happened at my house when _____ .
I help my family by _____ .

Story Titles
The Unwelcome Change
Dad's Dinner Delight
"Real" Life

Family Fun
Art and Language Arts

Remind the children how the family in the story enjoyed playing board games together in the evenings. Also discuss the importance of the little girl finally telling her family how she felt about her mother going back to work. Give each child a 9" x 12" sheet of colored construction paper and a 1" square piece of tagboard to make a game board. Invite children to trace the 1" piece of tagboard on the construction paper to make a path of squares traveling from a starting point to a finish line. Encourage children to color the squares, add comments in the squares, such as "take an extra turn," and draw colorful decorations around the path. Children may want to design their game board around a theme. Give each child a copy of the "Family Fun" reproducible on page 83. Invite children to cut the cards apart. Encourage children to take their game board and the cards home to play the game with their family members. When playing the game, each family member must choose a card and answer the question before rolling the dice and moving his or her marker on the game board. The game will encourage family communication and fun!

Create a Cafeteria

Language Arts

The little girl in *The Terrible Thing That Happened at Our House* did not like eating in the school cafeteria. She said the lunchroom smelled and all the yelling gave her a headache. Divide children into groups of four students each and invite each group to create a cafeteria that they would enjoy going to each day. Give each group three 12" x 18" sheets of construction paper and a sheet 4" x 18". Invite groups to use the first 12" x 18" sheet to create a poster advertising the lunch menu for a day in their cafeteria. Children can draw pictures of the delicacies as well. Have the group use the second 12" x 18" sheet to design a poster explaining four important rules to follow when using their cafeteria. The group can use the last 12" x 18" sheet to create a special cafeteria machine. The machine may be a special dispenser, a video game, or a clean-up robot. Invite each group to coin a unique name for their cafeteria and write it on the 4" x 18" banner. When the groups are finished with their cafeteria creations, encourage them to show their posters to the class and describe the benefits of their particular lunchroom.

Sock Sort

Math

One of the jobs the children in the story did to help around the house was to sort and fold the laundry. However, there was a slight problem—the socks didn't always "come out right." Show children the picture in *The Terrible Thing That Happened at Our House* that shows the little boy holding a pair of unmatched socks. Give each child a copy of the "Sock Sort" reproducible on page 84. Invite children to sort the socks by coloring or decorating each matching pair so that they look identical.

Be a Science Teacher

Science

The mother in the story went back to work to be a science teacher. Give children an opportunity to be a science teacher for the day. Ask each child to prepare for his or her debut as a teacher by going to the library and finding a simple science experiment to demonstrate for the class. Or, have a supply of reference materials in the classroom from which students can choose an activity. *Science Fun for You in a Minute or Two* by Herman and Nina Schneider (New York: McGraw-Hill, 1975) is a good source of simple, quick demonstrations of scientific principles. After students have chosen an experiment, assign each student a day in which he or she will be offering the day's science lesson.

Family Fun

Cut the cards apart and use them to play a game with your family.

What is your favorite color?	If you could be any animal, what would you be? Why?	What would you like to learn how to do?
What is your favorite day of the week? Why?	What makes you feel sad?	What makes you angry?
Where would you like to go on vacation?	What was the last thing you laughed about?	What would you like to change about yourself?
What do you do that you wish you didn't have to do?	If you could make one wish, what would it be?	What is your favorite book?
What is the best present you ever received?	Who do you admire? Why?	What would you like to build?

Sock Sort

Find the socks that match and color or decorate them so they look the same.

 3 + 2    10 - 8    9    1

 7 - 6   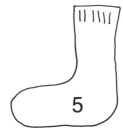 5    4 - 1    7

 3    5 + 4    2 + 2    2

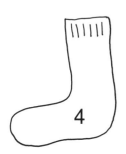 4    6   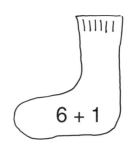 6 + 1    10 - 4

Families © 1991 Fearon Teacher Aids

The Terrible Thing That Happened at Our House

Maggie and the Goodbye Gift

Written and illustrated by Sue and Jerry Milord
New York: Lothrop, Lee & Shepard, 1979

Synopsis

Maggie has no idea what it means to be "transferred." She soon finds out when she and her family leave their friends behind and set off to a faraway place filled with "strangers." Maggie wonders how long her family will be sad and lonely, until she remembers the goodbye gift. The gift begins to work magic and soon the "strangers" turn into "people just like us."

Introduction

Ask children to think about what it would be like if they were asked to leave all of their friends and make new ones. Encourage children to name some good ways to make friends. Invite children to listen closely as the story is read aloud to find out how Maggie and her family make friends in their new neighborhood.

Critical-Thinking and Discussion Questions

1. Maggie was excited when her mother received a gift from her best friend, Alice. Maggie said that when someone gives her a gift, she always feels happy inside. How do you feel when someone gives you a gift? What are some occasions when you have received gifts?

2. Maggie and her family were moving to a new place. Things they saw on the trip were new and exciting. Their new house was beautiful. And yet, they were still very sad. Why do you think they were so sad, even when they had so many good things around them?

3. The family missed the people they loved. The people in their new neighborhood were "strangers" to them. How do you feel when you are around people that you do not know very well?

4. After Maggie opened up all the cans, the family was forced to find people to help them eat all the food. They began knocking on doors and talking to the "strangers." The goodbye gift started to work magic. How do you feel when you meet someone new? Is it hard for you to talk to them? How do you begin a conversation with someone you would like to be friends with?

5. Maggie knew just how to help Milton when he told her that his family would be moving soon. Have you ever been able to give a friend advice or help them with a problem because you had been through the experience yourself? When? What help did you offer?

Creative Writing Starters
Language Arts

When I meet new people, I usually _____ .
I was very sad the day my family _____ .
I think it would be fun to move because _____ .

Story Titles
The Friendship Factor
The Magic Gift
New Friends Behind Strange Doors

The Magic Gift
Language Arts

Maggie and her family had a problem—they had no friends in their new neighborhood. The can opener turned out to be a "magic" gift because it helped them make friends and solve their problem. Encourage children to think of some problem that they would like magically solved. Invite children to think of a gift that could be magically used to accomplish the purpose. Give each child a copy of "The Magic Gift" reproducible on page 89 and a 3" x 5" card. Have each child cut out the gift box and the bow. Invite children to draw a picture of the magical gift on the 3" x 5" card (lengthwise) and glue the bow to the top of the card. Using an X-acto knife cut the slit as indicated on the top of the gift box for each student. Encourage children to use the lines on the front of the gift box to write a paragraph explaining how the magic gift works and what problem it solves for them. Children can insert the gift in the box by sliding the 3" x 5" card in the slit so that the bow sticks up at the top.

Furniture Frenzy
Language Arts

The furniture was all jumbled up when the movers unloaded the big truck inside Maggie's new house. Give each child a copy of the "Which Room?" reproducible on page 90. Have children cut apart the worksheet on the dotted line and then cut out each picture square. Encourage children to decide in which room each item should be and glue the pictures in the correct columns.

Label Lookers
Health

Maggie and her family had supper with the entire neighborhood using the canned food Maggie had opened with the new can opener. Invite

each student to bring their favorite canned food from home. (Bring a few
extra cans of food for students who are unable to or forget to bring a can.)
Encourage students to take a careful look at the labels on each can. Help
students compare the ingredients, nutritional information, and calorie
count for each food. Make graphs on the chalkboard to display and
analyze some of the information. For example, make a graph showing the
sugar content of the canned foods. Explain to students that ingredients are
listed in order of quantity. The first ingredient listed is the ingredient that
is most prevalent in the can. Invite students to look for sugar in the ingredients on their cans. Graph the results. Categorize the cans by food groups
(meat group, fruit and vegetable group, milk group, bread group). If there
are no cans or very few cans in a certain food group, speculate why.
Discuss preservatives and look for them in the ingredients. Donate the
canned food to a needy organization, open the cans and have a potluck
luncheon, or have the children take the cans back home with them at the
end of the day.

Super Salutations

Social Studies

Maggie and her family had to say goodbye to their friends when they moved to a new neighborhood. Saying goodbye is a universal concept, though spoken in many languages. Present ways to say goodbye in other languages. Use a map to point out the countries where each language is spoken.

sayonara (Japanese)

auf weidersein (German)

adios (Spanish)

au revoir (French)

ciao (Italian)

The Magic Gift

_____
_____
_____
_____
_____
_____
_____
_____
_____
_____
_____
_____
_____

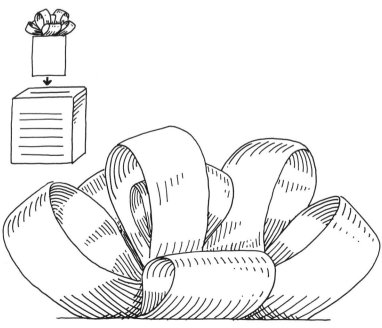

Cut out the bow and the box. Draw a picture of a magic gift on a 3" x 5" card. Glue the bow to the top of the card. Use the lines on the box to write about your magic gift. Slip your gift inside the box.

Maggie and the Goodbye Gift

Which Room?

Cut apart the worksheet on the dotted line. Cut out each picture.
Decide which room each item belongs in and glue it in place.

LIVING ROOM   **BEDROOM**   **KITCHEN**

- -

Maggie and the Goodbye Gift

Families © 1991 Fearon Teacher Aids

The Quilt Story

Written by Tony Johnston and illustrated by Tomie dePaola
New York: G.P. Putnam's Sons, 1985

Synopsis

A handmade patchwork quilt is Abigail's prize possession. It gives her comfort when everything around her seems uncertain. The quilt becomes a faithful friend and she finds many uses for it. A generation later, Abigail's daughter finds the old quilt in the attic. With a little repair, it is like new and Abigail's daughter finds the same comfort and warmth in the well-loved quilt.

Introduction

Ask children what makes them "feel at home." Ask children if they have ever felt uncomfortable in a new situation or in a new place. Invite children to listen closely as the story is read aloud to find out what makes Abigail "feel at home."

Critical-Thinking and Discussion Questions

1. Abigail used the quilt her mother made for her in many ways. She used it to keep her warm and she used it as a tablecloth for her tea party. What are some other ways Abigail used her quilt? Can you think of some other uses for the quilt besides the ones mentioned in the story?

2. Why do you think Abigail felt sad when she moved to her new house? Everything at her new house seemed unfamiliar to her, except for her quilt. Have you ever been in a situation where everything around you was new? How did it make you feel?

3. Abigail's daughter loved the quilt as much as Abigail did when she was a little girl. Do you have anything at your home that one of your parents or grandparents loved as a child? What? What possession of yours do you enjoy so much that you would like to save it so that your children could play with it someday?

4. After the quilt was very old, it was in need of some repairs. Abigail patched the holes and put in new stuffing so it would look "like new." Do you think it is possible for something to look "like new" when it is very old? Why or why not? Have you ever tried to repair something that was very old? Were you successful?

5. The quilt comforted both Abigail and later her daughter when they felt sad, lonely, or frightened. What gives you comfort when you are sad or frightened?

Creative Writing Starters
Language Arts

I wish my _____ could be made "like new" again.

I feel at home when _____ .

I would/would not like to move because_____ .

Story Titles

Mystery in the Attic

A Lonely Time

Welcome Home

Cinquain Sentiments
Language Arts

Write a cinquain together as a class about Abigail's quilt and how special it was to her. The first line of the cinquain could be "quilt." The second line should be two words that describe a quilt. The third line should be three words that describe an action associated with a quilt. The fourth line should be four words describing Abigail's feelings about her quilt. The last line is one word that restates the word "quilt." After finishing the cinquain together, ask children to think of something they own that is as special to them as the quilt was to Abigail. Give each child a copy of the "My Cinquain" reproducible on page 95. Encourage children to write individual cinquains about a possession that is very special to them.

Paper Quilt
Art

Children can make a beautiful patchwork quilt using paper squares.
Give each child a 6" square of white paper and invite children to design
a colorful pattern or picture. When the squares are completed, display
them all on a bulletin board. Alternate each child-designed square with a
6" square of solid color.

Name Banners
Art

Abigail's mother stitched Abigail's name into the quilt. Point out to
children how our names make us each special and unique. Ask children
if they own anything that has their name printed or stitched on it. Give
each child a 9" x 12" sheet of construction paper to make a name
banner. Have children begin by writing their names in big bubble or
block letters on the sheet of paper. Provide glue, glitter, yarn, and
construction paper scraps in a variety of colors. Invite children to make
their names dazzle. Encourage creativity and originality. Fold the top
edge of the sheet of construction paper over one inch. Run a piece of
yarn under the fold and tie the ends together. Staple the fold down and
use the yarn to hang the banners.

Falling Stars

Science

Abigail's mother stitched falling stars on the quilt she made for Abigail.
Abigail saw a falling star as she looked out her window at the winter
sky. Ask students what they think a falling star is. Give each student a
copy of the "Falling Stars" reproducible on page 96. Invite children to
read the paragraph and fill in the blanks choosing from the words at the
top of the page. Children can use the number code to decipher the word
in the last sentence to discover what a falling star really is.

My Cinquain

_____
(1-word title)

_____
(2 words to describe the title)

_____
(3 words to describe an action for the title)

_____
(4 words describing your feelings about the title)

_____
(1 word about the title)

Name _____

Falling Stars

Choose from the list of words to complete the paragraph. Use the number code to complete the last sentence and discover what a falling star really is.

light   gases   glows   star
tail   hot   metallic

A "falling star" is a bright streak of __ __ __ __ __ seen briefly in
                                                       1 2 3 4 5

the sky. The streak of light is not caused by a __ __ __ __ actu-
                                                           6 7 8 9

ally falling. A "falling star" is a chunk of __ __ __ __ __ __ __ __
                                               10 11 12 13 14 15 16 17

or stony matter zooming through the sky. The air friction makes

the flying matter so __ __ __ that it __ __ __ __ __. As it whizzes
                           18 19 20   21 22 23 24 25

through the sky, it leaves behind a trail of hot __ __ __ __ __.
                                                  26 27 28 29 30

This trail causes the "falling star" to look as if it has a __ __ __ __.
                                                          31 32 33 34

> A "falling star" is really a __ __ __ __ __ __.
>   10 29 7 11 19 9

Families © 1991 Fearon Teacher Aids

The Quilt Story